Keys To A New Life

by

Daniel Boone

Keys To A New Life
by Daniel Boone

ISBN: 978-93-59394-53-4

Published by

DOUBLE 9 BOOKS

2/13-B, Ansari Road
Daryaganj, New Delhi – 110002
info@double9books.com
www.double9books.com
Tel. 011-40042856

This book is under public domain

ABOUT THE AUTHOR

Daniel Boone was an American pioneer and frontiersman. He was born on November 2, 1733, and died on September 26, 1820. His adventures made him one of the first American folk heroes. He became well-known because he explored and settled Kentucky, which at the time was west of the Thirteen Colonies. In 1775, Boone cut the Wilderness Road through the Cumberland Gap and into Kentucky, despite opposition from American Indians who used the area as a hunting ground. He started Boonesborough, which was one of the first places where people spoke English west of the Appalachians. By the end of the 18th century, more than 200,000 people had followed the path Boone had marked to get into Kentucky. Even though not everyone remembers him well, Boone is still a famous person in American history. He was a legend in his own time, especially after a book about his travels came out in 1784 and made him well-known in the United States and Europe. After he died, many brave tall tales and works of fiction were made about him. His real and made-up adventures helped build the classic American frontier hero of folklore.

CONTENTS

1.
The Power Of Ideas

IT IS a fact that no truth is of any use without a method of application. So in this book is given a method of use or application of the general principles of the truth which Jesus taught.

The reader will discover that this book is most original in that it departs from the usual in metaphysical writings and deals only with those phenomenal manifestations of mental power with which the author has had personal experience.

Some clear definition of terms used is essential so that all may get the same picture of the idea presented. Hence I shall make use of the word Spirit. Spirit is the power which animates you and causes *life* to flow through you. There is no mystery in either the word or in what Spirit is. And above all things it has nothing to do with death or any degree of death.

Spirit is that which is *eternally and actively alive*. This Spirit, then, is that which occupies every atom of matter, every point in space, and is *actively alive in every instant of time*. It is the energy of life which we call God and is *now present, here*.

Spirit is that energy which causes life to *move into expression*. In short, it is the power behind the thing (or thought). In this book, Spirit is to mean in every instance that which is causing the reader to think-—now. It is like the electricity which gives the power which makes the street car move. It is not the car but the power which moves the car.

All manifested fact and all demonstrable science comes from an idea in some one person's mind—thus, all truth goes through three stages of development: First, men say that it is not true; second, they declare that it is "blasphemy" or is a violation of the divine will or is hostile to religion; third, they say that it has always been known and dig up some ancient philosophy which they claim has always taught it.

Here then we see the method of Divinity in dealing with Its creations, particularly man—you. Each individual has a point of mental contact with God (whether or not he knows it or believes it). By virtue of this "point of contact" with the Cosmic Presence within his own mind, each individual may receive ideas (or an idea) straight from God but, before this idea becomes a demonstrated fact of life it must pass through the process stated above. If you tell it to any man he will say that it is not true; he will declare that it is hostile to religion or tradition. After it manifests itself, he will say that he "knew it all the time".

And here again we see that the story of Jesus of Nazareth is an outpicturing of this very process. Jesus, through mental acceptance of his oneness with God, received an idea from God; men said that it was a lie—then they said that it was hostile to their religion—then they crucified him. Now they say that the same truth he taught had always been taught and every ancient superstition the world ever knew has been brought forward seeking to impose itself upon this truth and claiming that it had always been known to the ancients; and we have the spectacle of so called Christians abandoning their churches to follow after those who trade upon these ancient philosophies and superstitions.

This writer has experimented with every known philosophy and presents his thesis to the reader in the utmost confidence and assurance that no other teachings extant are as easy to use and as profitable in their use as the teachings of Jesus Christ.

Simple enough to be understood by a child, strong as the rock and as positive and instant in their action as the radio waves, they act upon the heart and mind of him who makes use of them, as music acts upon your radio receiving set and bring the harmonies of heaven into actual manifestation in the life and affairs of all who are faithful to the principle involved.

Jesus taught first the general principle of life, explaining that life was a mental phenomenon, then he taught us how to *use this* general principle specifically to meet our needs—first our own individual needs, then the needs of others who touched our life at any point.

The name and achievements of Jesus Christ have been associated with religion, and religionists have concerned themselves with life after death specifically and with moral and social antagonisms until the real practical use of the mental laws he taught have been so disguised as to be almost unrecognizable.

When we consider the teachings of Jesus in terms of life after death, their import and practical application seems far removed from us. It is to present the actual demonstrable method of *use* of the general principle he taught that this book is presented.

This book is distinctly different from any other you have ever read—different because all the other books you have read dealt specifically with the personal equation—with your relationships with other persons. This book ignores everybody on earth save you—the reader. It is written for you and specifically *to* you who are now holding it in your hands. It is about *your* mind, and its purpose is to reveal clearly the fundamental laws which govern the action of your mind.

When you go to school and study arithmetic you do not demand of your teacher that he give you all the figures you shall ever need—you are satisfied to learn the principle, then you feel confident, certain that, regardless of what figures you run across, you can handle the situation. This is exactly what I shall do in this purely personal talk with you in this book.

As this living, vital truth and its method of use and application is presented to you, be prepared to find your own mind going through the process of phenomenal reaction described on the preceding page. Your mind may at first reject the idea on the ground that it is not true. Next, your mind may reject it on the ground that it is "blasphemy" or that it is not what constituted authorities have always taught or that it violates your religion. If this takes place, observe your mental reaction and know that it is perfectly normal, and recall that what is herewith presented has nothing whatever to do with tradition, religion, (yours or another's) or with any other person.

Recall to your mind the fact that you have, in your hand, a personally written textbook on how to handle and make use of the Mental Laws which govern all mind action. Recall to your mind that all you are seeking in this personally written document, is to learn how to apply the principle. Be certain that once you have trained your mind to *apply* and make use of that principle, that you will find yourself the absolute master of any situation which can possibly arise in your life.

First know that the Mind, *per se*, that is, the substance of mind, is, in and of itself, static, motionless, poised, always and ever in perfect equilibrium. Next, know that an idea introduced into that mind substance moves by and of its own power and volition, and *always* reproduces itself under a cosmic necessity, expressed in the Bible thus: "Increase and multiply and replenish the earth."

In short, an idea introduced into Mind does not have to be pushed about; it moves by virtue of the life within itself just as a seed planted in the ground does not have to be dragged up—it grows up in spite of the resistance of the earth, by virtue of the life within itself and by cosmic necessity to fulfil the law of "Increase and Multiply".

Next, know that we are not dealing with theological theories, metaphysical speculations nor abstruse or mysterious parts of things. We are talking about *your* mind and the laws which are eternal, cosmic, unchangeable, and which make the one who rightly applies them master of himself and circumstances, here on earth, now.

Recall to your mind constantly that we do not care what will happen to us when we "die" because we know that this life in which we have our being *cannot die.* Hence, death is nothing but a phenomenal change of the substance of that Mind and in reality is a birth, just as it was a birth when your physical body came out of your mother's womb.

Next, know that your mind, that is, your awareness of being alive, is born out of this Mind—that this mind *is* the Holy Mother of the Scriptures, that the laws governing its phenomenal expression follow exactly the laws which govern conception, gestation and birth of the physical body—with one difference. In the subject we are new studying, it is the *idea* which is immaculately conceived (in your mind) which goes through the process of "gestation" in your mind and finally comes forth into manifestation as part of yourself.

Next, you are to know that all the peculiar phenomena of objectified life you see around you expressing as unsocial conduct as between man and man and nation and nation is the result of the wrong application or misuse of the laws which govern mind and that there is positively no escape from any unhappy condition, whether it be poverty, sickness, unsocial conduct or what not, save the right application of the laws which govern mind. Then, with this knowing, understand that each individual is compelled by a cosmic necessity to learn, experiment with and actually use the right principle in his own mind. It is nothing anyone can get from another—all one can give to another is what the teacher gives the pupil—a knowledge of the principle and a method of using the principle. This is what I am doing personally to and for you—recall, this book is a privately and specially written textbook, written for *you.*

Next, know that there is absolutely no answer to any of the eternal questionings of the human heart save those answers which automatically result from the right use of the laws which govern mind. Every question your heart or mind ever asked is answered in and by virtue of the use of the right laws which govern your mind.

Next, know that there is positively no such principle in these mental laws as "right" or "wrong", in a moral sense. Right and wrong have nothing to do with mental laws any more than right or wrong have anything to do with the principle of mathematics. Get this idea firmly fixed in your mind at once.

There are two basic actions of any idea—Basic because Cosmic laws with which man cannot interfere govern the movement of all ideas. One is attraction, causing cohesion of ideas, families, groups, institutions, governments or races of peoples. These all come under this one law—and its social name is LOVE. Love is a Cosmic phenomenon and positively *not* a personal thing between a man and woman, father and son, or mother and daughter.

Love is the name of the cohering, attracting action of an idea moving in mind.

Next, you are to know that mind has its laws just as electro-magnetism has its laws, just as physics has its laws, and that the laws of mind are just as scientific as those laws of electro-magnetism or physics. We are dealing with an exact science when we deal with the laws of mind.

Love is a Cosmic phenomenon and is the attracting *power* of the idea as it moves in mind. It is the exhibition of the desire of that idea for expression in form so that it may exhibit itself and enjoy its own livingness.

Hence, the Cosmic phenomenon of love is what causes the tiny cell to increase and multiply in the womb until the idea of life contained in that one cell has a form in which to enjoy and experience life and to exhibit itself *as* life.

The Cosmic phenomenon of love is what causes ideas to increase and multiply in your mind and this increase is the Cosmic urge operating under the divine command; "Increase and multiply and replenish the earth".

And this brings us to the consideration of the "Word". It is stated: "In the *beginning* was the Word". A word is a sound and represents an idea. Hence, we see a relationship within our own living experiences for the idea then becomes the spirit or motivating power which causes the sound (word) to become flesh—exhibit itself in form. Whether you are seeking to attain eternal life, health, wealth, companionship—whatever it is—it can come into being only by and through your conscious use of this creative principle. "Ye are gods" said Jesus and, being a god, you are a creator and are to create what you desire—not try and take it away from someone else.

Hence, when an idea begins to function within your own mind you are mentally an observer of the phenomenon of the actual action of Spirit— it is become a personal living experience of your own. You need ask no questions and seek nowhere else for information, for you are in the actual presence of all there is either as to meaning, substance or activity of Spirit.

You are not the Spirit—but you are a witness to its presence and activity. As ideas begin to take form in your mind and your own mind witnesses the fact, you know that it is not you, the personal man, that is doing the "works" but that it is the Spirit within. That is, it is within your own mind and consciousness.

You are, in such a case, an observer of the actual living presence of God and are beholding Him at his work. The Father worketh hitherto—and I work, said Jesus. You are furnishing the conditions which *permit* God to do his work. You are as necessary to God Almighty as he is to you. He could not be conscious of being alive were it not for you—YOU, to whom this book is addressed and who are reading this word. This WORD is that which is "in the beginning" and the idea back of it (in me) is its Spirit, the Spirit which gives it life and makes it a living, vital, positive and powerful exhibition of the "re-birth" of God-conscious-ness in you.

Recall to your own mind the fact that we are studying the Cosmic laws of mind for the purpose of learning how to rightly use them in the business of living, right here on earth, in the commonplace everyday affairs which environ us and which face us daily, hourly—to be used in the actual experience of being, thinking, creating, achieving.

We are dealing with exact laws, irrevocable laws, immutable laws, cosmic laws, laws of mind, laws the right use of which will make you master of yourself and of circumstances.

If you are sitting on the shady side of your house and wish to get into the sunshine on the other side of your house, you know you have to get up and move. To move you must *be* somewhere, and go from that place to another place.

In dealing with mind, the same holds true. If you are in any state or condition of being which is unsatisfactory to you and wish to go hence, you have to mentally move from where you are to the other place.

When dealing with mind, we are seeking to move mentally away from the place we now are and into the place we desire to be. The place we wish to get away from is the confused mental condition of human thought, and the place we desire to go is the harmonious mental state called heaven.

We already know what the human thought atmosphere is like and have had all of it we care for —but the place to which we desire to go will have to be created within our own minds by the right application of those mental laws taught and exemplified by Jesus.

Do not be afraid to let go of your preconceived ideas. They resolve themselves into nothingness at last and are to be discarded and dissolved as they have done their work and are no longer needed. Let go—begin to learn to actually *trust* the Infinite out of whose substance you have been formed.

There is nothing to fear. I shall not let you descend, I shall raise you with resistless will, for "I AM" that in you which is eternally one with that poised, balanced, Substance of Mind which is God.

Resurrection is the law of this supreme Mind of which you are the living Word—made flesh that It might exhibit Itself and manifest Itself. Nothing can defeat this omnipotent law of resurrection. Nothing in heaven or earth wants to defeat it. Every law, force, power, intelligence in the universe is eternally cooperating with it.

You are to learn how to make personal use of it.

You shall no longer be a victim (?) of circumstances; you are to become a *maker* of circumstances.

Relatively, there is as much space between the cells of your body as there is between the stars in the heavens. Your body is only relatively solid; actually and in fact you are a state of conscious awareness in Mind, an actual, manifested, formed embodiment of Mind—of God. Ideas act upon and move every cell of your body every second of time and you may learn to cause this motion to conform to the order and harmony of the universe you behold about you. This is called health (harmony).

When this idea came into my mind, I resolved it into the word by the process of accepting (mentally) It as true of me.

Then an old hymn came to my mind. This universe of which I am a part is operated by order, hence the tune of the hymn came to me in a split fraction of time just when it could be used. And here is that idea resolved into the Living Word.

These are my words to the old tune:
Steadfastly proclaiming my indwelling health,
Steadfastly claiming God's increasing wealth,
My mind and my body is healed and made whole
And I enter the kingdom of peace in my soul.
Steadfastly relaxing my hold upon things,
Steadfastly seeking the King of kings,
The spirit of God in the midst of me

Makes me one with God in the midst of thee.
For the Spirit which binds us all as "one"

Is given to us by the risen Son,

And steadfastly proclaiming the promise true

Makes you one with me and I one with you.

This idea (word) sang itself into every cell of my body, thrilled it with vitality and power and livingness. This song was a divine harmony (to me) because it came forth out of my own substance through a process of thought originating in my mind's acceptance of a Cosmic fact of my being. It was nothing I borrowed from another.

So, here, we have the method of applying the creative law of mind, taught and demonstrated by Jesus of Nazareth who, because of his use of that law, was called the Christ, the Master, the Anointed One. I salute the Christ in you.

2.
The Mystery Of "The Word" Made Plain

"IN THE beginning was the word."

This has always been made a very great mystery. We have read the text, heard it discussed from the pulpit, read books of interpretation, but ever and always these things have seemed to mean to your mind and my mind, something which God did long long ago—before the world was formed. Never has anyone revealed to us that the statement was a scientific formula of creation, available for us to use now.

Also we have heard it said that there was no beginning, and therefore there will be no end; and this, too, has seemed too impossible a statement to be accepted as a usable fact of life about us.

Creation, Life, is a continuous performance, and in fact there *is* no beginning and no ending of either creation or life but there *is* a beginning of specific manifestations of being. Likewise there are endings of these specific manifestations of being, but Being Itself is not involved in the beginning or ending—only the specific fact is involved either in a beginning or an ending. Herein, we begin to get a usable fact from this scientific formula with which we may deal definitely for our own ongoing.

There *was* a beginning to your physical manifestation and there will be an ending to it, but Life (within you) is not involved in either the beginning or the ending save as a living experience of specific fact.

You went to a movie last night. The play had a beginning and an ending, but you were not in-volved in either the beginning or the ending, save as the bounds and circumference in time which identified it as a living fact of experience to you. That is, your own Being, the life which is in you, was not limited by either the fact of beginning or ending.

Here, then, we begin to get some sense out of that hitherto hopelessly mysterious text: "In the beginning was the Word".

If you are ill, impoverished, lonely, or suffering from any unhappy condition, and wish to be free from it, then it is evident from the above interpretation of this scientific formula that the new condition you desire must start with the "word". A word is a sound symbolizing an idea. Scientifically, if you wish to rise out of illness, poverty, or unhappiness there must first be the idea in your own mind of health or abundance. This idea is the beginning as far as your freedom is concerned; that is, this idea of a better condition must find its beginning as an idea in your own mind.

This is not some mystery which God performed in some mystic past before the worlds were. It is an action in your own mind of creative thought and is to be used by you to bring about the changed condition. This idea in your mind is like the raising of the curtain at the show last night; it is the "beginning" of a new living experience and to you.

It is a beginning of a new experience—but does not in any wise limit or restrict the continuity of your life. You, conscious of the God power of your own creative thought, say (within yourself), "Let us create". You image forth or image in your own mind substance the picture of the man you are to be.

You mentally "write" this mind picture of what you desire to become, just as I am now writing these letters and words on this sheet of paper. And just as your mind is acted upon by virtue of the Spirit and Life of these words you are now reading, so the substance of Mind, *per se*, is acted upon or immaculately impregnated by your mental picture. This mother substance, being thus impregnated, the process is begun whereby the *word* is in the "beginning" of bringing forth a new experience of life for you and to you.

Here, then, we see how and why there must be a "word" in all "beginnings" for, "Without the Word was not anything made which was made". There is no mystery about it at all; this scientific formula of mind action is just as reasonable as the formula whereby we solve an algebraical problem.

As long as our minds seek amongst the thoughts of other persons for a basis of creative activity, we miss the mark of our high calling as self conscious beings—gods in the making; but if we understand that this Holy Mother Mind Substance is within us and can be acted upon by our own mind with the same ease and simplicity as we have hitherto acted upon human ideas, we discover a source of wisdom within ourselves—we come into conscious contact with the "Father within".

We begin to perceive that we may bring about new conditions and new experiences in our lives by the same mental process we use in planning a new dress or a new house. First is the desire for the dress or house, then the mental picture (image) of the dress or house. In short, "In the beginning is the Word".

The creating of new health, new prosperity and new experience all along the line is no more mysterious than the bringing into our lives of a new dress or a new house and is done by the application of the same mental law. We do not have to learn a new thing, we merely need understand the right use of what we already know.

We do not have to destroy anything through denial; we see that those conditions which we no longer desire fall away by virtue of their own disproportion when we stop thinking of them. We need concern our minds only with the "word" or "image" of the thing or condition we desire to bring into manifestation.

We need, in short, only make use of that mental activity which Jesus referred to as righteousness, that is, make a right use of the mental laws we have been using to our disadvantage all the time. This right use of this mental law will bring new conditions into our lives as living experiences, and is what is termed righteousness. We are righteous or *right* because we no longer hurt ourselves or others by and through our ignorant use of the law of life.

We have to *think*. This thinking process is nothing short of talking to ourselves silently and alone.

In order to make right use of the "Word" and bring about those desirable conditions which promote my own and others' happiness, I agree (within my own mind) to make a continuous effort to *think* health instead of sickness; to *think* prosperity instead of poverty; to *think* good instead of evil; to *think* of blessings instead of curses; to *enjoy* the sunshine instead of worrying about the night. As I make a mental habit of such thoughts, I shall no longer carry scandal and tales of evil about my neighbor. Thus I shall make my own living experiences conform with the universal harmony and order which govern the universe of which I am a part. I will no longer talk about poverty to others; I will encourage instead of discouraging others; I will be a friend instead of an enemy; I will be cheerful instead of blue and depressed.

I will think deeply about things. I will be more grateful for the great achievement of Edison whose mind and its creative power gave me *light* for my house. I will be consciously grateful to Marconi, Tesla and all others who have made right use of the mental law of life and given me the pleasure and profit of radio. I will be most grateful for the achievement of the lowly Carpenter of Nazareth who, making a right use of the mental laws of life, gave a light to my mind which makes me the master of circumstances and makes me free.

I will no longer take things for granted. I shall be grateful for the idea (Spirit) which animates men's minds and makes it possible for the "Word to become flesh," for the idea of Cosmic wholeness to resolve itself into a clear concept in my own mind which thus becomes the living word of health and is (to me) the beginning of the actual manifestation of health as a living experience to and for me.

I shall daily take an inventory of the miracles of modern life and understand that these all came forth out of the womb of the Holy Mother Substance because of the power of the Word finding expression through the mind of man. I shall begin to awaken to a realization of my own rightful place in the Cosmic scheme and understand that I, too, have the same power to use the Word rightly and thus create and bring into manifestation new and better conditions for myself and those I love.

I realize the absolute truth of what Emerson meant when he wrote: "The mind that is parallel with the laws of Nature, will be in the current of events and strong with their strength".

In all material or objectified manifestations of life, we see the exhibition of force, one thing acts upon another to force or coerce a reaction.

This is exactly the opposite of the method you are to use in the future. The primal Substance, (Holy Mother), MIND, responds to your impelling idea but positively will not respond to any effort at compulsion. Any mental force or effort at coercion meets with instantaneous failure.

It was a knowledge of this fact which made Jesus teach the law of love.

You may *impel* but cannot *compel*.

Hence, I do not teach denial or affirmation which resolve themselves into force or coercion. Rather I teach you what Jesus taught—calm, quiet, sane, rational, thinking processes.

No one ever saw Life try to force or coerce the growth of a rose. The action of life and beauty in a rose is silent, sweet, easy, lovely. It is an *im*pelling outworking of a cosmic fact, and in nowise a *com*pelling action.

Even the medical profession is beginning to learn this fact; doctors are becoming mere spectators of natural and cosmic facts of life. They no longer seek to force or coerce nature in the human body. They look wise, say nothing, and let nature take its course; then they know they have an assistant that knows what it is about.

Hence we are enabled to see the rational and wise provision of Life that when any condition is to be changed, the individual desiring this change has within himself all the power, and has available all the substance, necessary to originate and complete that change as a living experience of his own life, thus becoming a witness of the truth.

We see that we are dealing with Mind, and that to get the maximum out of life we must learn the mental laws which govern life and rightly apply those laws to our own thinking processes.

We see that the instrument that sobs the "loser's blues" so despairingly can just as easily respond to a triumphant march. We understand that the piano; in the corner which will wail La Miserere will also more joyously play "See the Conquering Hero comes". We see that our own mind is the instrument upon which we have been playing, either the sweetest symphonies of beauty or else the discords of life.

Understanding this mental law of the Word, we see that there is no confusion regarding our statement of the Cosmic fact of wholeness when that which is manifesting is sickness. For, we are to *create* as a personal, living experience, a condition of health. We are to move from where we are to where we wish to go by the use of that mental law of creation given in the text: "In the beginning was the Word".

If you will read the first chapter of Genesis, you will see that God created a perfectly formed world and filled it with life out of waste and void. This chapter (of Genesis) is a description of how to use the mental laws Jesus demonstrated.

Hence if I were ill and wished to become well, I should make use of this mental law and begin to calmly and sanely and quietly think myself into a right relationship with the Cosmos instead of succumbing thoughtlessly to what appeared to be me. I should not waste a second's time as to whether or not this or that were true—I would use the law to be free of that undesirable condition.

If there were a "fear" anywhere in my mental makeup, I should read often the 136th, 138th and 139th Psalms until the idea they contain became a part of my normal mental activity.

The individual, through rightly using the mental laws taught by Jesus, can free himself from all fear. The Psalms to which I refer above are mental medicine to heal the mind of fear.

Now read the 145th Psalm—and THINK.

Even as a pigmy East Indian directs and controls a two ton elephant and makes him work for his master, so man, through the right use of mental laws, can direct and make work for him the creative power of the universe. But, it responds to fear as quickly as it does to any other mental attitude.

3.
How To Give A Truth Treatment
To Yourself Or Another

VIOLENT mental movements are always stampedes within the substance of your mind. This is true whether the violence is intended to move you forward positively or backward negatively. Calm, deliberate, quiet thinking of and about an idea is normal to creative processes. When your mind Works along those lines, your mind is in harmony with the cosmic processes, or, as so aptly said in the words already quoted by Emerson, your mind is "parallel" to nature and nature's strength vitalizes all you think and do.

An idea of the harmony and order and the universe, *thought* into relationship *with* the thinker, relates the thinker *to* that harmony and order. And this Cosmic harmony and order is more powerful than fear, and once established banishes fear forever.

This kind of thinking has been called "going into the silence" and by various other names, but none of the names given the process is as revealing as to call it just exactly what it is—a simple, sane, calm, quiet thought process.

It has been called "concentration" which is exactly what it is not. When one CONcenters, one contracts. This true thinking process is expansion — expansion of the mind's substance, expanding it until it gets free from the limited circles of petty worries and fears and expands to where it begins to touch the larger dimension of being which I have called order and harmony.

Calm, deliberate, purposeful thinking thus relaxes the mind and the body and permits the flow of Cosmic energy (harmony and order) to function easily and without Congesting limitations, outward from the center into life in its wholeness.

This is giving yourself a treatment. You do not put your attention upon your body, nor any part of your body, your attention is taken entirely off your body and placed upon an idea which relates you, as a self conscious being, to the sum of life which we term God, You give another a treatment in exactly the same way. You do not try to force the other into anything, you think of him calmly, quietly, sanely and easily in the same manner that you thought about yourself. That in him which knows truth recognized the fact that you are recognizing it—and thus it is confirmed; finds an avenue of expression (expansion) itself in and through that one.

Remember back to when you enjoyed perfect health and you will readily recall that at that time you did not put your mind's attention upon your body. Healing results in getting the attention of the mind off the body entirely. Your self identification with disease will outgrow itself if your mind will give it a chance—even an egg can outgrow its identity. And it requires no "treatment".

The method of calm, quiet, sane and effective thinking just described has been called yet another name. It is the best name yet given to it, and that was the name given by Jesus who called it: "Seeking the kingdom of heaven within." In this calm, quiet, deliberate thinking process is nothing of stress, strain or burden; it is a mental recognition of and a mental acceptance of a Cosmic fact of life about the thinker, and he soon finds that he lives in a very friendly universe, every law of which is kindly and beneficent. The thinker thus engaged soon perceives that every agency in the universe was intended to serve him in a friendly manner and that there really is nothing to fear.

One of the best established and best known mental laws in our academic psychology is this: By repeated thinking of and about anything, we arrive at a mental acceptance of it. When women first began wearing short skirts, there was much resistance to the idea, but by repeated thinking of and about it and repeated seeing it brought into action, the whole world arrived at a mental acceptance of it.

A boy in school cannot learn history or mathematics if his mind is focused upon football. If he wishes to become proficient in history or mathematics, he will have to think history and mathematics.

You cannot mentally accept health as long as your mind's attention is focused upon your sick body.

Our mind's action sets into motion universal and friendly laws of Being which are kindly and beneficently inclined toward us. Our spoken word liberates substance and causes it to flow into and makes visible the perfect image and likeness in which we are created. Our spoken word, spoken consciously and definitely and purposefully from a mental certainty, releases a power that is greater than either we as thinkers or the word itself.

Thought must be done first. This mysterious "kingdom of heaven" is nothing any more mysterious than your mental acceptance of the divine order and harmony of the universe and your recognition of yourself as being part of it and a beneficiary of its beauty and wholeness. After you have done this thinking until it is rational to your mind, then your word is the *word of power.* The same word spoken without the thought process is powerless.

Merely thinking and stopping there, however, fails to bring about the desired results. The idea once established must be used. You cannot remain a failure in this universe of order and harmony, save by self consent. The moment you think you have failed, you stop using your ideas. It is the *actual use* which produces results.

The divine order of creation according to the Genesis story indicates that God is a God of action. He started something—He is eternally starting something; he started it with gracious initiative, with kindly and loving thoughts toward the whole of it including you. He is still loving and kindly toward you, but that fact must be accepted by you mentally, then used to make itself seen or felt in your life.

One of the disciples asked Jesus, "Where abidest thou?" Jesus replied: "Come and see." And the story goes on to relate that "He came and abode with him." No locale is mentioned—it was a state of mind. The disciple put his mind's attention upon the Cosmic wholeness and when he looked at the same thing at which Jesus was looking, the disciple *"saw"* the same thing Jesus saw.

If you will calmly, quietly, sanely, easily think (come and see) the cosmic wholeness which environs you, you will also see what Jesus saw— the Father, an orderly, harmonious universe operating under kindly and beneficent laws which were given for your especial benefit and for your personal use.

A knowledge of your divinity is no earthly good to you as long as it remains in your head. Put to use, it means the difference between bondage and freedom. A dollar in the bank to your credit is no earthly good to you, but used, it becomes a power which you wield to attain your ends.

The idea you have of and about what you are doing is what inspirits it. It is that process called, breathing into it the breath of life, that which makes of your work a living, breathing, vital thing. If you think about your work as drudgery and of yourself as a slave, your work (no matter how well done) will take on the gray drab color of a slave and be dead and inert and without life and vitality.

If you think about your work as a self conscious god creating a thing of beauty and power and enduring loveliness, then that work takes on the sunrise glow of Cosmic beauty and becomes alive and vital and is inspirited.

That is, the idea (thought) back of the work is "the Spirit which giveth life?" The actual "work" may be identical—one is alive, the other dead.

A Supreme Life, Love and Power is eternally protecting you. And, there is nothing to fear.

All the equipment there is in the universe is contained within yourself,

Use is all that keeps it hidden from view. Fear is all that keeps you from using it.

"Have no fear", said the Carpenter's boy from the little town in Gallilee. If his mind could make such tremendous use of the fearlessness, of conscious acceptance, so can yours.

To mentally accept the Cosmic wholeness is to mentally see and accept your own relationship to It—which makes of you the "son". To all who "believed" on His name gave He the power to *become* sons of God.

4.
What Are You Doing With The Teachings Of Jesus?

PLEASE imagine, in beginning this chapter, that you are sitting alone, in your home, reading a personal letter written especially for you and specifically to you. This is a personal address and concerns you and you alone, like a letter from your sweetheart.

The purpose of this personal address is to put you in possession of certain eternal truths, the use of which shall make you master of yourself, master of your destiny and a partaker of the divine grace of God as promised by Jesus Christ.

It has been the habit of readers of metaphysical literature to seek some mystery. There is no mystery here—mystery never met a human problem, paid the rent or bought any clothes for the baby. What we are seeking is the mystery reduced to comprehension and usability.

Your mind has accepted teaching from every conceivable source, but your mind has refused to let the simple teaching of the Master Mind—Jesus —find a resting place in your mind or heart. What are you going to do with this amazing man? What are you going to do with the amazing picture he painted in the consciousness of the world?

You cannot escape him. You cannot escape meeting, face to face the question—what are you going to do about Jesus the Christ?

You may be a Russian atheist, a Japanese Shintoist, a Hindu Buddhist, an Arab Mohammedan, you may belong to any race, color or belief, but at this time there is an awakening in the mind of humanity which demands that each individual answer this question definitely for himself.

No other's words will suffice; Jesus said: "Heaven and earth shall pass away but my words shall not pass away". No other man ever dared make that statement. The words of Jesus the Christ are unique in that they stand alone in human consciousness as a mind picture of certain mental laws which will, when taken into the mind of the individual, save, redeem, heal and prosper him.

It is not required that you settle in your mind what I have said, or what any other man has said, but it *is* required of you that you decide for yourself what you are going to do with the words Jesus said. His words are established as the definite, orderly, Cosmic fact of life to each individual and, as stated in Scripture, sooner or later to him every knee shall bow — to his words all must come for that living refreshment which satisfies the soul and which conforms to the orderly processes of the cosmos.

Christ consciousness is a realization in your mind of your oneness with God. Its power is not limited to time or place nor is it bestowed upon favorites who comply with any man-made theory. It is, like sunshine, for anyone who will step into it and partake of it.

You are to study and practice with the ideas Jesus taught until your mind becomes saturated with those ideas, and you are to do this *for the love of accomplishing that degree of mental comprehension which he had* and not for the purpose of getting a healing for your stomach-ache or release from your poverty.

His teaching about this matter is very plain and very easily understood, even by a little child: "Seek ye first the kingdom of God; and all these things shall be added unto you. And your Father knoweth ye have need of these things".

In over a quarter of a century of metaphysical practice, I have not encountered a dozen persons who came to me for help who came for anything except to get rid of a pain, to get rid of a husband or a rival, to get rid of poverty or to gain some power over another person.

In your study of the teachings of Jesus, be perfectly sure that if you want results you will have to study and apply yourself for the sake of finding a conscious relationship to God within; then you will see health, abundance and joy and happiness added as a matter of course and without conscious effort on your part. For just as Jesus stated: "Your Father knoweth ye have need of these things".

This is not accomplished by asking a practitioner to "hold the thought for you", nor by getting a practitioner to speak the word for you. Remember that the practitioner is in the same relationship to you as the teacher is to the child — an instructor. The growth is normal, gradual and accrues through your own efforts to understand the principle involved and through the constant practice of that principle in the business of every day living.

Does this do away with the need of practitioners? By no means! Never in the history of the world was there such a demand for teachers of the Christian doctrine, never was there such a demand for practitioners; but these must teach the words of Jesus Christ, as found in the Four Gospels of the Christian Bible, and stick to them exclusively, to be worthy of the name of teacher of Christianity.

The development of this Christ consciousness may be compared to tuning in a radio receiving set: When you first turn on the electric current, your radio does not instantly respond, it requires a minute or two for the coils and tubes to get warmed up and saturated with the electrical current and its power. So your mind, like a radio receiving set, tuned as it has been all your life to the negations of the world, shows no visible or identifiable result when first you start your studies. It takes time to get the old lazy half dead brain cells warmed up and saturated with the vitalizing power of the living words of Jesus Christ. But soon, if you persist, the results will show forth and you will have the conscious experience of knowing how to consciously tune your mind in to the Christ consciousness, just as easily as you tune your radio set in to a favorite station.

In summing up this little personal talk between you and me, let us recapitulate: There is but one true teacher of the truth as taught and exemplified by Jesus Christ, and that is the Spirit of Truth which he promised would be our Comforter. That Spirit of Truth is within you—you, I mean, to whom I am now personally talking—but you have not recognized this Spirit of Truth. You have been recognizing Tom, Dick and Harry, but not the Spirit of Truth within yourself. But I have been recognizing the Spirit of Truth within myself and within you. So, if I should speak the truth to you now in this little personal chat, then the Spirit of Truth within you will recognize this truth and there will be a response within you that will be a witness to the fact that what I have said to you is that truth.

Thus Spirit to Spirit doth speak and, in truth we commune one with another and the living word becomes established as between thee and me and we two agree on this thing which touches us here on earth and then it is established as a fact by the Father because of this unity of our understanding and agreement. ("If two of you shall agree as touching anything that they shall ask, it shall be done for them of my Father which is in heaven".)

Thus we have a living experience that bears witness to the fact that there is but one mind, the Mind of God. Each of us is one with that Mind in that each of us is a focal point of self-conscious oneness with it, hence we are one with each other. We see how easy it is for you to love me, your neighbor, as yourself because in this oneness we are the same self, the self of self-conscious Being, which is the God in us.

Jesus said: "That they all may be one; as thou, Father, *art* in me, and I in thee, that they also may be one in us". (John 17: 21)

We realize the power of consciousness and subjugate our conscious mind to nothing and submit to nothing save the Father within.

This idea of subjugation is to be gone into very thoroughly in your own mind and thought out to its logical conclusion. We see this every day; it is well established in the human consciousness. The American Medical Association in its scientific propaganda to retain its power and dominion says repeatedly, through its journals and health institutes and clinics, that no mind can function perfectly except through a perfectly healthy body, thus again subjugating consciousness (mind) to the flesh; Jesus taught that the flesh was subject to the mind, not the mind to the flesh. His resurrection proved that he was right.

History also proves that Jesus was right, for the most stupendous mental and intellectual attainments have come from men and women whose flesh was deformed, torn by pain or hideous with distortion.

Steinmetz, the electrical wizard, was a deformed man; Paul himself was a squint eyed little runt who was subject all his life to epileptic fits; many of the world's greatest minds have proven that imperfect flesh can function the perfect mind. Jesus alone stands out as the perfect flesh with the perfect mind. Usually the perfect flesh is at best a prize fighter or football end who lasts ten years then fades into oblivion.

The mental giants of the ages have been those whose flesh was so imperfect that of necessity they turned to mental attainment for comfort.

This one point learn and believe as taught by Jesus: *All* things in heaven and in earth shall be subject to the power and dominion of consciousness, your mind.

"All power has been given unto me in heaven and in earth" did not refer to physical prowess, but to mental power and poise and understanding.

5.
What Jesus Taught About Your Conscious Mind And How To Use It

GOOD evening, friend and fellow-journeyer.

Again we meet to have a chat about consciousness—the operation of the conscious mind, your conscious mind.

At this point I shall talk about and make use of the term soul. It is not necessary that I give to you the positively last word or ultimate truth about what constitutes the soul, it is only necessary that your mind understand what I mean when I use the word so that we may come to an understanding of the subject.

Much is said in church circles about "saving the soul", and Jesus himself used the term saying: "And fear not them which kill the body, but are not able to kill the soul: but rather fear him which is able to destroy both soul and body." From this it is evident that the word had a meaning to him and that there were powers operating that could destroy the soul.

Let us consider a moment: Toward what is all our educational effort directed? Is it not toward the education and perfecting of the conscious mind? What ails this world anyway? What ails you? Is it not a lack of understanding in your conscious mind? If your conscious mind were aware of how to solve your problems, then would you not solve them? Well, then, to me it looks as if the conscious mind of man is the soul. It is that which is to be saved. Since your conscious mind is an expression of the universal Mind of God, then your mind or soul is immortal, because God's Mind is immortal. Hence comes the expression—the immortal soul.

Then it is your soul or conscious mind that is to be saved; saved from what? Ignorance, evidently, since that is all that ails it; since ignorance of how to think, ignorance of the conscious thinking mind of man, is all that ails the world, then obviously the thing to do is to teach or instruct the conscious mind, thus saving the conscious mind, or soul.

Let us deal then in these discussions with the conscious, mind or, if religiously inclined, you may call it your soul. It is not necessary that this definition be correct. As long as we two agree on this definition, then we can talk and understand each other.

There are those who have the power to destroy the soul or conscious mind. All who teach the necessity of subjugating the conscious mind have such power. Those who teach that it is evil, that it is limited or helpless, those who teach that it is unable to cope with living experiences—all these have the power to destroy the conscious mind or soul. Jesus warned us to beware of them. Those who could only destroy the body could not touch the conscious mind, or soul. But those who destroy the mind also destroy the body.

This is an important point for us to consider, this idea of there being a power which is able to destroy the soul or conscious mind. Jesus did not say that this power was "evil", he merely mentioned the fact that there was such a power.

Let us turn to electricity for an illustration, for in it we have a perfect symbolism of the subject. You have a general idea of what electricity is; it is an invisible energy capable of doing certain things under certain conditions, such as light your house, drive your carpet sweeper, ignite the gas in your automobile, rotate the fan which keeps you cool, etc.

Let us say that in New York we have the electric light, in Chicago we have the carpet sweeper, in Denver we have the ignition in the automobile. Here we have several different objects, each in a widely separated district, but all operated (made alive and active) by the power of electricity.

Now we all know that although the objects are all different and are widely separated as to space and time, the power which animates or operates them is one and the same.

You may destroy any one of these objects at any time but the electrical energy itself is in no wise harmed. Further, the electrical energy can never be depleted, nor diminished, for the more demands you make upon it the more energy flows forth. Again this electrical energy is impersonal in that it works for a Chinaman, a Frenchman, a Russian, and an American with equal power and willingness.

Life, Mind, is just like this electricity and our physical bodies are like the different objects we have named. It is the life that animates them and destruction of the body in no manner hurts or interferes with the mind or power which is really us.

It is obviously the conscious mind or soul that must be saved. According to the teaching of Jesus, the Man of Light, this saving process is, in its last analysis, up to each individual; something each has to do for himself with the help of the living, indwelling Christ.

Hence the work of Jesus was an educational work, and this educational effort was put forth for the benefit of the individual; it was directed especially and specifically to *you*. He spoke words of truth and light into the human consciousness, words of such transcendental power and beauty that they are eternal, for he said: "Heaven and earth shall pass away but my words shall not pass away." His words were sounds symbolizing the idea he set forth, the idea of the unity of your life with Life itself, with the Life of the Father, stating specifically to you: "Ye are a god and the spirit (life) of the Most High dwelleth in you." He was saying as you might to the electric fan or carpet sweeper, "Ye are of use and the spirit (life) of electricity dwelleth in you" — stating a fact about that which was invisible yet perfectly obvious to one who knew what it was that animated the electric fan or the carpet sweeper.

He knew what it was that animated his own physical body and the brain it held, just as the electrician who manufactures electric fans and electric carpet sweepers knows what it is that animates them and makes them appear to be alive and active.

Material science in delving into the scientific aspect of material nature has discovered that so-called dense matter is in reality only relatively dense. The General Electric Company has developed a high voltage tube which photographs an object through six inches of solid steel. The action of this high voltage tube upon the solid steel reveals the fact that the atoms of the relatively solid steel are as far apart, relatively, as the stars in the heavens and that great spaces actually exist between the atoms which compose this apparently solid substance.

Hence we find material only relatively solid, exact science confirming step by step the more exact science of mind as taught by Jesus of Nazareth.

Abbe Lemaitre, the distinguished churchman and astronomer of Belgium, says that the universe was originally one vast atom. He bases his speculation upon the very latest theory of the world's greatest scientists, the quantum theory, the very last word in material or physical science.

But Sir James Jeans, the great British scientist and the author of many scientific books, says that he thinks the universe is not one vast atom but rather one vast thinking brain, and that our world is just one tiny cell within it. Thus we see religion becoming scientific and science becoming religious, one substantiating the other.

Once the idea is conceived and established in the mind of the thinker that the universe is a vast brain and that every atom of matter, including the cells of our own body; that every point in space and every instant of time is animated and made alive by this one supreme, infinite Mind which is God; that we, each one of us, are an important and essential part of this one Mind's expression— we get an entirely new outlook on life and begin to see the simplicity and beauty of Jesus' teaching.

"I and my Father are one," is not, then, something true only of the man of Galilee, but he merely stated it for each one of us to use for ourselves, saying that it was true of everyone.

And to substitute this belief for the old belief was to "save" our immortal souls. Tradition is the greatest destroyer of the conscious mind or soul, for tradition is based upon and exists by virtue of this posit:—That nothing can be true or happen unless it is true and has happened in the past. Life itself by its very nature is constant and continuous change. A baby just born is different within the first ten minutes of its existence and it changes every instant of time not only as long as it lives in its body but afterward.

Change is the law of life and so tradition becomes life's greatest enemy, the greatest destroyer of the soul or conscious mind.

It was this that Jesus meant when he warned us against those who had the power to destroy both the soul and the body. He did not refer to forms of conduct called "sin" as taught by preachers, he taught that to resist change was to destroy the possibility of growth, hence destroy the soul. Suppose the infant a day old had a mind and it could resist change and growth. It would remain forever an infant. This would interfere with the order and harmony of the whole and as a result this resistant object would have to be destroyed for the benefit of the whole. The power which destroyed this object would not be satanic or evil, it would merely be the operation of one of the forces which make change possible.

Today we get a new concept of our relationship to God—intelligent Mind. Supremely intelligent Mind animates every atom of matter, mineral, vegetable and animal. Every cell of your body is animated by this one, supreme Mind of God.

The posit of physics that: "If there be any force which acts, it can only be known by virtue of the fact that there is something upon which it can and does act," is true of mind. If there is a spirit in man, if it be true that "ye are gods and the spirit of the Most High dwelleth in you," then the only possible way in which you may become aware of the fact is that there is something within the range of your living experience for that spirit to act upon. It is the action of the Spirit within upon the condition as it exists which brings about that phenomenal experience which we call healing, release from bondage, wealth from poverty, beauty from ugliness, maturity from ignorance, etc.

Instead of calling the present estate evil, instead of quarreling with it or seeking to escape it or have it removed by some practitioner, let the student lay hold of it with delight, as the carpenter lays hold of the lumber, and begin to build that which he desires or considers desirable.

Material science has only recently proven that the cells of our body are separated by spaces as vast by comparison as the space which separates the heavenly bodies. Yet Jesus knew this two thousand years ago without the aid of material science. How did he know it? He must have been apprised of the fact through the impartation of wisdom directly from the Mind of God to his own conscious mind.

I repeat, this discovery is a recent one. Yet this recent proof makes the fact no different and no more true than it was two thousand years ago. That which is true is eternally and unchangeably true; discovery and proof of the fact in no wise alters the fact that it has always been true and will always remain true.

Your mind, accepting the teaching of Jesus as true, will make a discovery and you will have actual living experiences which will reveal it to you, yet it will not change the fact that it was true then and will ever remain true. The daily application of this idea to your every day living will change your life entirely. You will find yourself communing with the indwelling Father often and lovingly and joyously. You will find this indwelling wisdom acting upon your conscious mind or soul to save it from its ignorance; you will find yourself guided into new efforts, new adventures, new growths, new prosperity, new health—newness and ever more newness—because you accept this truth as taught by Jesus, that "I and my Father are one," and Paul said: "Know ye not that ye are the temple of God and that the Spirit of God dwelleth in you?" (I Cor. 3:16).

You will approach the task before you in that consciousness of mastery and power, utilizing the inspiration within to act upon your present environment or condition to bring about the change which conforms to the universal progress of life itself.

We are transformed by the renewing of our mind. We let the mind which was in Christ Jesus to be in us, for we think the same thoughts he did, we acknowledge the Living Presence of God in our midst and, since God is greater than we are, since God is all powerful, since God is eternal and perfect, then our minds begin to contemplate and see as true of us the things that we see are true of him and "I and my Father are one" in fact.

6.
The True Way To Liberation From All Burdens

THE WHOLE scheme of metaphysical practice, the whole scheme of redemptive power, the whole science of mind and the whole argument leading to liberation from bondage resolves itself inevitably around the fact of God's Omnipresence. The immediate presence of God is in every atom of matter, every point in space and acting every instant of time.

There positively is no rest for the weary soul, there positively is no peace for the troubled heart, there positively is no healing for the body and there positively is no liberation from bondage to poverty until the conscious mind consciously casts the burden, the whole, entire burden of its life upon this Living Presence.

Once it is rationalized, once the conscious mind so adjusts itself to this fact that there is no argument *within* against it, that nothing in the *without* can affect the conviction, this inner conviction of God's Omnipresence washes the entire man clean; the divine Alkahest descends like a silent benediction, the soul receives a purification as though it had been drenched with clean sweet summer rain; the peace that passeth understanding takes possession of that man and all those things he so eagerly sought and which so persistently evaded him are added, full measure, heaped up and running over.

Thereafter he moves by the divine right of godhood; kingly in the gentleness of conscious strength, rich in the certainty of limitless substance, above pain, above strife, above the storms of turbulent hearts, he moves with the mark of the Spirit upon his brow like a royal heraldry. Wherever he walks he heals; without thought or effort his very presence heals the hurts of broken flesh, soothes the tempests of hatred and enmity. He walks as did Jesus, a witness of the glory of God.

Before this takes place the last vestige of belief in duality must be eradicated; the last vestige of belief in any power to oppose this Omnipresence of God; every word which means sin, sickness, evil, poverty must be cast out of the mind by the mental act of choice, and through the exercise of this choice substituting the thoughts of God's omnipresence for the thoughts, words and ideas which are to be cast out.

The work that is to be done is to be done with your own mind. It is exactly like housecleaning— old worn-out things are to be thrown away, burnt up, given away, disposed of in some manner; every nook and corner is to be cleaned, new wall paper, new curtains—new furnishings throughout—so these old ideas, ideas to which your family and neighbors cling with tragic tenacity—must be left behind. You can never do it if you try to take some loved one along with you; you can never do it if you try to make your family understand. There is no one who can understand save that omnipresent God within you which is the Spirit of Truth.

For this reason it is a silent work—silent because it is thinking which cannot, by virtue of its disturbing power, be translated into words directed toward your neighbor. Your silent thought is directed toward the indwelling omnipresent God and your conversation is with Him and Him alone. All the so-called systems of attracting health, wealth and love are nothing save the silent, sincere, persistent willingness to accept these things from God as a matter of course; yours by divine right, Yours, not because you strive or struggle; yours, not because you chastise yourself with many observances; yours, not because someone in authority asks them for you—but yours by grace, yours by virtue of the fact that God loves you and desires you to have them and is constantly bestowing these things upon you.

That time and space are the fourth dimension of Being is well established, and that objects or things are projections in time and space is well known. The process by which things emerge from unformed Spirit into time and space is life's mystery. We may see it, enjoy it, use it—but we do not understand it.

A very significant fact of science lies in the truth that the two greatest forces on earth which man uses most are things of which he knows absolutely nothing. These two things or forces are mind and electricity. No one knows what mind is, its source, its destiny; no one knows what electricity is, its source, its destiny. Yet, by complying with certain laws of mind man has conquered the earth, the seas and the air. By exercising his mind he has penetrated the secrets of nature, spanned chasms miles wide, sailed to the depths of the sea, and ascended to the edge of earth's atmosphere and in every case recorded facts of use and interest to him there.

Jesus taught that by observing certain mental laws, laws of recognition, acceptance, use, that Mind, God's omnipresent Mind, would find an avenue of expression through that thinker and that this expressing of the inner spirit of man, this outpouring of the one, omnipresent Mind of God through that individual, would do all that person's work for him, would wash him clean of the silliness, ignorance, doubt, fear, hate and envy of the world mind.

You need actually know no more about Mind, *per se*, than the woman who uses a carpet sweeper knows about electricity in order to put its silent power to work for you, but you must observe very definite laws before it will do its work without hurting you.

The infinite, primal Substance of Supreme Mind fills all space and is the base of every formed thing and is the substance and life of every active thought or idea. It flows in and through you this minute, ever active, intelligently active, purposefully active; it is friendly toward you. The Psalmist, seeing this, said: "I know the thoughts I think toward thee, saith the Lord, thoughts of peace and not of evil".

This infinite primal Substance, is what scientists are discovering and naming "electronic activity," etc. The laws which cause this equilibrated Substance to spring forth into activity as thought and action and as form is the subject of the thesis we call the Bible—it is the divine mystery we call God, it is the objective toward which all mental activity flows naturally; for there is something in the heart of mankind which desires and longs with an infinite longing to come into conscious Oneness with this Mind which each knows to be its source.

A sense of protecting love fills the mind and heart of one who understands the stability and unity and omnipresence of this one primal Substance and knows that it is God, Himself.

Dr. Jesse W. M. DuMond has made spectroscopic photographs of the movements of electrons and writes of his experiments in the press recently saying in part, "The photographs of the movements of electrons show that these agile infinitesimals dance in orbits at speeds up to 90,000 miles a second. Steel, copper, wood, any seemingly stable and opaque substance, is in reality a seething whish of velocities.

"There is something refreshing to the imagination in the thought of all this winged invisible fire of energy. Buildings grow old and dingy about us, the pavement of the street is worn and greasy with the passage of innumerable automobiles.

"Our own hands arid feet seem, at times, to be heavy with the weight of years and troubles. But then comes this thought of the underlying wash of clean electrons, basic elements of Being, tiny elves of Cosmic dew, moving in their ceaseless tides back and forth, round and round, within all familiar objects, and within our own beings,

"It is to such gigantic movies of the mind that modern science invites us. One leaves the show comforted and invigorated?'

Dr. DuMond is saying nothing new in this article just quoted. Jesus said the same thing, in different language, two thousand years ago. The Psalmist sang of the self same fact twelve thousand years ago. Now science confirms the masters of mind whose songs have held the heart of mankind toward all future with hope and courage and strength when the nights were black with ignorance.

Jesus taught us that if we identified our minds with these Cosmic facts of life that we should be alive more abundantly, that this invisible Substance was obedient to our strong word of command and responded lovingly to the action of faith upon it; that it received the pictures or images man made in his mind as a kodak film receives the picture or image of the object in front of the lens when the shutter is opened. Like the camera, the mind must be "opened" to the idea and to the fact as true before any image can be made upon the mind. It is here that faith in the omnipresence and the goodness and the friendliness of God finds its greatest field of activity.

The beginning of wisdom is the casting away of everything save essentials. There are certain essentials in the use and application of mental laws. The first of these essentials is to understand at once that the thinker (called variously the "I am", the spirit, the indwelling Master, the Christ Mind, etc.) can do all things in consciousness, and that consciousness is his one and only field of activity. He is to work in and with his own mind.

The technique of this mental work lies in building up such confidence in the Substance upon which the mind is working that the thinker feels that it (the Substance) is taking form just as surely as the carpenter can see and know that the lumber he is sawing, cutting, fitting and nailing is assuming form and shape.

This is done through the imaging faculty, the ability of the thinker to imagine himself as being that which he desires to be, and by building into that image the corresponding activities which go with that character and in the consciousness that when this is done, man, (the thinker), has reached his absolute limit of effort, that at this juncture he reaches the unknown, and that here he must leave his structure with that unknown process which projects that form into the fourth dimension of time and space and thus makes of it an actuality.

This transfers any problem from its formed aspect back into consciousness, the universal solvent, back into that universal sea of pure Substance, into which all formed things finally must resolve themselves. And while here the problem will reform from the undesirable into the desirable through the action in consciousness known to the thinker as thinking definitely toward the desirable rather than submitting to the undesirable appearance as formerly.

One is to understand that this process of thinking is creative, is in harmony with divine law, is the exercise of man's inherent god power and god privilege, and that he is to build into the process the conscious certainty that he is using a Cosmic law of creation and that back of his mental processes is all the power there is—the very power of God in action; and that there is, permeating every point in space this universal and limitless Substance, waiting to be acted upon by his mind that it may come under the law of expression and show itself forth.

It is essential to build into the consciousness the surety that this one universal Substance is positively impersonal—and that it is a unit—-that it is this all pervading Substance which unifies and makes of all diversity one thing and substance; and this knowledge that he is acting upon the one and only Substance when he thinks, teaches man the science of love and the absolute necessity for it; for the injection of hate or bitterness or envy into his thinking processes introduces into the forms one creates, the elements of their own destruction.

As Jesus stated, love is a Cosmic phenomenon and is the law of creation; this is so because of a necessity. The universe could not persist were it not for the cooperative forces which govern it. The instant any opposing or destructive power became active it would disturb the equilibrium of the whole, just as the moment you find a pain in your body it disturbs the poise and balance of the whole man, spirit, soul and body. So, in order to promote the integrity of your own physical and mental welfare, you seek to obey the laws of life as far as you know them; hence the application and use of love in thinking processes becomes the most important subject with which the thinker has to deal.

When man, in his thinking processes, uses only love as a force or power to project his imaged forms into being, he will find that every force, power, element, and substance of the universe will rush to him obediently to do his will, because this is that action of the thinker's mind which cooperates to create and at the same instant maintain the equilibrium and poise and balance and integrity of the whole. In it there is no hurt to anyone or anything; in it is no restriction of the perfect liberty of anyone; in it is nothing of harshness or hardness; in it is nothing of tightness or tension; in it is nothing of envy, of bitterness, of hatred or animosity toward anyone or any thing. The thinker feels and realizes that he is dealing with a friendly substance, obedient and willing to do his bidding. He realizes that he lives in a friendly universe therein every law is designed for his benefit and that back of the phenomenon of his being and consciousness is a vastness of like character which is "greater than I", and, while like unto him, is and must forever remain unknown save as it reveals itself little by little as he consciously cooperates with it in perfecting all that his life touches, bringing forth beauty, order, harmony, peace, love and good will.

To a thinker thus engaged there is revealed the fact that he need no longer look to persons for anything. He can see and feel the God quality in them so, instead of addressing himself to Mary Jones, he addresses himself to the God in Mary Jones. The results are amazing, remarkable, miraculous, for the God in Mary Jones has been there a long time waiting for recognition but none save the sons of God can recognize it, that is, none save thinkers who have recognized the one Universal Presence and established it firmly in their own consciousness.

First, then, we see the thinker resolving all things, problems, facts of objective life back into consciousness, dissolving their seeming and then re-forming them into desirable conditions, then recognizing the reformed condition as already existing in those about him, thus fulfilling the law as stated by Jesus: "***whatsoever things ye desire***believe that ye receive them".

The thinker realizes that all his work is done in consciousness, his own consciousness. He is to know that he can go no further and must leave all results with the law he has thus invoked.

He leaves others alone, he ceases from the futile and senseless effort to change other persons' minds and busies himself with changing his own mind.

As he practices this process, failing utterly and often but persisting faithfully, he finds himself finally where the law he is seeking to use reveals itself clearly to him. He finds that the law itself does all the work, that with his own consciousness he has only to furnish the conditions and that this calls into action something higher and greater than either his own mind, his own ideas, his own powers or his own word. He realizes that he has released Cosmic forces and substance, and as a farmer planting a seed does by that act release Cosmic life into new expression, the thinker discovers that his mental activity has released Cosmic life into action and that the law itself carries that mental act into complete fulfillment. There is no effort, no burden —and no credit assumed; Man stands as did Jesus, a witness to the glory of God, God present, now, active and alive and doing His perfect work.

7.
The Keeper Of The Keys Of Life

THE AVERAGE person being a non-thinker, having formed his opinions of life from what appears before him as form and shape, gets the impression that all action is accompanied by noise. Thinking, being a quiet process, one imagines that nothing transpires during thought processes. Silent thinking to him is devoid of power, produces no action and therefore is useless.

When he first undertakes to study mind and the silent processes of thought, and is told that in this still, calm, quiet place lies supreme power to shape his destiny, he is rather dubious to say the least. He demands something with action, something with noise, something that explodes into fireworks; he wants things to move, he wants miracles to be performed to prove to him that the proposition is true. In short, as Jesus stated, he is "seeking a sign". But no sign is given him. He has his choice—he can return to his boiler factory of noise and confusion, he can return to the world of form and shape and disappointment as many times as he chooses, but before he can get any results from the silent power of his own Spirit, he will have to have faith that he *has* such a silent, quiet Spirit, and he will have to have faith that this silent Spirit has power to move up to time, events and things and change them to his liking. He will even have to have faith that this silent power within has more power than all the noisy, blustering, self assertive powers of the world he has known. Finally, he will have to have faith that this secret, silent, invisible, inner power is the Supreme Power of the universe which nothing can oppose.

The thinker learns that there is a quiet place in his consciousness, that within his own mind is a place comparable to the country, a place of rest and refreshment where he may go as often as he pleases and find that rest he so badly needs and where he will not only escape the nerve racking sounds and motions of daily life but where he will find healing for his addiction.

No one but the thinker may enter this place of rest and quietness for its gateway is the stillness and its portals are opened only to those who believe in the presence of the silence within. Hence, in educating your mind to have faith in the silent power of the inner self, it is first essential that you learn to contemplate the Divinity within your own being. This mental movement toward your source acts at once to calm the mind of its reactions to noise and motion and the first effect upon the neophyte is a sense of peace and rest.

This discovery that there is a divinity within you will never be made known to you by another. Others will name you many things, but never, under any circumstances, will they name you the son of God or see any divinity within you. No one would acknowledge Jesus as the son of God. They called him a son of the Devil, a blasphemer, a nuisance, but never the son of God—that was a title he gave himself. At the time he gave himself this title, he was talking to Peter (meaning faith in the inner self) and Jesus said at that time: "Blessed art thou", (for understanding this, that "I AM is the son of God") and "upon this rock I shall build my consciousness", and "I will give unto thee the keys to the kingdom of heaven: and whatsoever thou shalt bind on earth shall be bound in heaven; and whatsoever thou shalt loose on earth shall be loosed in heaven".

One who, through thinking, discovers that he is, of necessity, a son of God, is given a blessing; this blessing is an illumination of the mind. Practice with these new values, use of this new faith, places in your hands the key to life and makes of you *the keeper of the keys.*

Such a one realizes beyond argument that there is one supreme, omnipresent God permeating every atom of matter, occupying every point in space, and acting as life and love and power in every instant of time; that there is nothing before him save this Divine Presence, nothing behind him save this Divine Presence, nothing above him save this Divine Presence, nothing without him save this Divine Presence. That the very substance of his body, the substance of his food, the substance of his thought is all the substance of God—good, friendly, obedient, loving, powerful and wise.

He discovers that what he has always thought was thinking was merely permitting his mind and organism to be acted upon by noise, confusion, motion, that his supposed thinking was nothing but reactions to what happened in the without and that thought originates within himself, and that this quiet thinking about any subject is true meditation and yields its own reward.

He discovers that thinking is knowing God, if his thought be about or toward God; that thinking is the silver lining to the clouds of doubt; that thinking is the *spiritual* way; that thinking is the cure for care, the strength of action in its balance; that thinking is prayer; that thinking passes from intellectual knowing to living reality; that thinking brings trust, and quiet unshakable faith in all that is good and true. That thinking brings guided, intelligent action proceeding from a calm mind.

Think, then, if you would rise to realms of knowing and pure action. Think, then, if you would carry healing in your touch. Think, then, if you would walk strongly, unfalteringly and undismayed the rugged pathway of life.

For thinking is the "pillar of fire by night and the pillar of cloud by day" which guides all men to the promised land. Thought is the lark's heaven-piercing song at dawn. Thought is the beating of angel wings against the windows of the soul. Thought is an excursion to the borderland of the eternal. Thought is an exploration of all truth and is man's greatest adventure with God. Thinking brings the holy hush of twilight and the sunlit promise of dawn. Thinking causes the bursting of the seed in the stillness of the soil, the stirring and quickening within the womb which precedes new birth. Thinking breaks the chrysalis and liberates the soul to its joyous flight in sunlit fields. In thought we are resurrected in and with the Christ. Thinking restoreth my soul.

The thinker begins a systematic re-education of his mind. He no longer forms conclusions from the outer world and its accumulation of facts and traditions; he begins to form his conclusions about himself and life in general from within, from the Cosmic facts which are so obvious about life, love, faith, strength, courage, hope, newness, renewal and eternity. He begins to dimly see that these are principles which inhere in life itself and form the basis and the basic facts of life forever.

The thinker senses right from the beginning of his thinking processes, that life is a continuous awareness of being and that once any thinker identifies himself with Life, *per se*, the life of that thinker is secured in its continuity and growth in knowledge, understanding and unfoldment. He receives a baptism of inner light which reveals to him that he could not avoid healing wholeness manifest as his natural and rightful heritage; he knows that he could in no wise avoid the ever abundant provision made for the whole creation, he sees himself in an entirely new light and new relationship and knows that this new vision of him-self is his re-birth, that out of the chrysalis of time worn inhibitions he is unbound, the wings of thought carry him into fairer fields and he senses the freedom of his indwelling spirit which the world can never again bind with the foolishness it so profoundly calls wisdom.

If he feels a need of healing he knows that that very sense of need is his preparation to receive it, and gives silent praise and thanks for its forthcoming. His realization of the Infinite Presence gives him assurance of the fulfillment of any need. He realizes that in that Infinite Presence is the fullness of life, love, power, abundance, all things, since that Infinite Presence fills and activates every living form. He is filled with an inner and unkillable joy because that Infinite Presence is joyous in its expression of itself. In this Infinite Presence is ever and always a manifesting, unspoilable health and wholeness to which he is entitled as a matter of course. Healing to him becomes a joyous witnessing of the truth of his being. He enjoys its progress as a boy enjoys seeing some toy completed under his hand, as an artist enjoys seeing a picture take form and shape under his brush, or a director enjoys hearing a mighty symphony in sound under his baton.

Soon the thinker finds himself talking about health instead of disease; about prosperity instead of poverty; telling good news instead of bad news; mentioning his blessings instead of his misfortunes; encouraging instead of discouraging; being friendly instead of unfriendly; keeping silent instead of carrying scandal. In short, he soon discovers that his thinking has taken form in words and then, lo and behold, he finds that his words have taken form and shape as health and abundance.

He discovers that man is the product of his prevailing mode of thought and, just as the Bible teaches: "As a man thinketh in his heart so is he." He has proven the law as given by Jesus of Nazareth. Thus Jesus of Nazareth has been and is his Saviour from sin, sickness, poverty and death.

The thinker stops trying to get others to tell him what is wrong with him and begins to discover what is right with himself; he develops through his thinking processes an humble acknowledgment that he of himself can do nothing, but a sublime faith that the Presence of God within him can do all things, will do all things, desires to do all things for him. He discovers that his tasks formerly so odious and monotonous get themselves done with easy grace and undeniable power because he has silently turned the doing over to the indwelling presence of God; he discovers that his mind has become centered and poised upon an idea which is as solid as Gibraltar, as immovable as a mountain, as strong as a rock, as irresistible as the surge of the sea.

As soon as the thinker has taught his mind to accept God's living presence, God's wholeness, God's goodness, he finds that he has discovered the secret of attraction, that people begin to come to him for healing, to catch the warmth of the bright wisdom which sparkles in his new born mind, to bathe themselves in the freshness and beauty of his spiritual nature now emerging from its tomb and now resurrected into Cosmic consciousness.

He discovers that the power of attraction lies in the ability to accept. That all his former misery, poverty, sickness, fear, were attracted to him because he accepted them from the ignorance of the world; and that, by the self same law, he may accept health and abundance from God, they being attracted to him by virtue of his acceptance of them. This gives him the key to helping others. Again he discovers himself to be the keeper of the keys.

He knows that the "Keeper of the Keys" is he who has faith in God's Omnipresence.

He has also discovered that health and wholeness, freedom from cramping poverty, did not come because he learned to manipulate some mysterious law for his own benefit, but rather it came because he sought and found the kingdom of God within for its own sake, and that health and abundance have been added as a matter of course because health and wholeness and abundance belong rightfully and naturally to the sons of God.

The thinker has thought until he has related himself to the Cosmos; he has discovered the divine unity of all things. He senses the One Mind permeating every living form; so, when one, any one, comes to him for healing, he knows at once that this is a divine appointment, that the One Mind has brought that person to him because that One Mind knows that it can heal that person through him. It makes no difference what words he uses or what thought, it is always the right word or the right thought for that particular person in that specific moment of time. The thinker takes no burden, accepts no credit and acknowledges that the healing is complete in that instant of time. Thus he heals with undeniable power, because it is the indwelling Father who doeth the works. These are the fruits of thinking, and can be attained in no other way.

This idea of thinking which I am setting forth here is not an individual view of mine, neither is it some radical departure from the conventional. The thinker has ever been the "Keeper of the Keys", the thinker has ever been the master of life, the holder of the seat of power and the director of the destiny of mankind.

Individuals who know how to think effectively have distinguished themselves in history from the beginning. Thought processes, however, have undergone a most radical change within the past fifty years. This is the cause of so much talk and literature upon the subject of the mind in general and so much and such insistent reversion to the thinking methods taught by the Master Thinker of all time, Jesus of Nazareth.

Things and events which are recorded in the Bible as miracles are child's play in comparison with modern scientific achievements; and mankind in general now makes use of devices which he takes as a matter of course which outdo all Biblical miracles by one hundred percent. These modern miracles are the result of thinking on the part of first, one isolated individual, then the cooperative thought of many others who group themselves about that thinker's idea for the purpose of making practical use of the benefits that idea offers to humanity.

In this manner, we can easily trace the origin of the telegraph, telephone, wireless, radio, automobile, flying machine and other miracles too numerous to mention here. Man has lived in isolated communities where he maintained his own national, tribal or racial integrity by virtue of his power to fight, and so it was but natural that when science began to probe the secrets of invisible forces that man should divert these new found powers to the same line of effort and perfect himself in the art and science of war, and in the art and science of industry that his art and science of war might be backed by adequate productivity.

Little did man dream, however, of the depths of his mind and the limits to which it might carry him in this direction. But he is just now awakening to the fact that his next great scientific achievement must be in moral science, and that he has already progressed in the classical sciences far beyond his ability to use the products of his own mind.

In his probing of moral values and in his seeking for a method of readjustment that civilization may be saved from the destructive forces modern science has produced, man tries vainly to apply forces to the advancement of moral science. Here he is dismayed to discover that force plays no part in moral science and that the application of force, regardless of how high the motive, destroys the moral nature he seeks to protect.

Our next great scientific achievement, then, must be in the advancement and perfecting of moral science. That advance and perfecting process must be done through the individual, hence our educational institutions and our education mediums become the tools essential to this advance and progress; the tools are already built, perfected to a high degree. We are at present using this splendidly equipped machine to bring about economic disaster by the overselling of manufactured goods, and are also using it to create in the minds of the individuals of which Our nation is composed an inclination for more war. These same tools used as an educational medium to educate the individual, in a new moral sense could within two generations produce a race of men in all nations of sufficient moral stature to form a world state in which all nations might intelligently cooperate for the welfare of each other, with war abolished forever from the face of the earth.

The very foundation of our nationalistic educational systems lies in the hero worship instilled into the minds of school children by holding before their young minds great warriors as the nation's greatest characters; this can be changed and great moral characters substituted and yet the educational system need undergo no change from its present functioning. Florence Nightingale is a far greater character than Napoleon, yet she plays no part in school curriculum.

Man's mind, developed through thinking, has perfected the sciences of chemistry and physics to a very high degree. With these as his weapons man is wresting from an apparently reluctant universe her every secret and is codifying an exact knowledge of her secret forces which he is using more and more in every day living.

There is no limit to the achievements man may attain, there is no end to the path upon which he has set his inquiring mind; there is no diminution to his conquering spirit.

But for what shall man use this knowledge? To what end shall these secrets of nature be applied? To destroy himself, or to weld together into one cooperative body the whole of humanity?

There is no moral science equal in its fundamental facts to meet our present needs save that moral science taught by Jesus of Nazareth. But this science must be taken away from theological institutions, taken out of the hands of the church, wrested away from dreamers and the whole subject matter placed in the hands of exact science where it may receive the cold and even unsympathetic scrutiny of those minds which are trained to carry every experiment to its ultimate limit and find the answer only when the idea pursued has become a fact of everyday life available for the use and enjoyment of all.

The world has, today, a certain degree of intellectual and spiritual unity never known before. The harvest is ripe, but where are the laborers? This degree of intellectual and spiritual unity is the direct result of the use of what exact science has accomplished and in no wise is it due to any effort of the church; the very basic elements of the church are to divide and separate into factions and groups whereas, the very basic elements of science are to unify and bring together. The church with its thousand creeds produces a thousand separate non-friendly groups. Science through the radio produces one hundred million people of diverse groupings into one compact solidarity of thought and emotion.

Hence I say, that if we are to save civilization from the advance of classical science and the instruments of destruction which classical science has produced, the effort must be made by and through the medium of science. The new moral science will receive its first impetus through science.

8.
In Thought Lies The Destiny Of Mankind— Social, Economic, Moral

THOUGHT cannot be nationalized nor made the property of any nation, race, group or corporation. Therefore, thought is the one unifying element at man's disposal by and through which he may hope to build a better estate for posterity. Thinking thus becomes the most important matter before the masses today; for the masses are not thinkers yet—but have merely accepted the thought of their masters throughout the ages. Their masters, being individuals, can change their thought almost over night, but the masses are a more unwieldy group and it will take many years to change the general direction of mass thought to any appreciable extent.

Hence he who undertakes in ever so small a way to act upon the individual mind to the end that he may direct his thought to or toward world peace, the application of those qualities of being taught and exemplified by Jesus, becomes by virtue of that effort a mighty figure in the scheme of things. By that effort he is preparing the individual as such to lay hold of and make use of the one sure, safe though silent power which can and must save civilization from itself.

He is preparing the mass mind bit by bit, to accept and use what science produces, not to destroy but to conserve, not to separate but to unify, not to antagonize but to reconcile.

Imagine that every man, woman and youth in these United States had been individually trained to think in terms of peace when war was declared against Germany a few years ago. If not a man responded to the draft, what could the government have done about it? Nothing. America would not have engaged in war. What is true of America is true of every nation, for all nations are composed by and of human beings and all human beings can and do control the situation when they know how and are not afraid.

The "Keepers of the Keys" have hitherto been the jailors of mankind. Their keys have been keys to the jails of ignorance and limitation wherein they kept the masses securely locked and by which they kept them enslaved.

These same keepers must change their keys, must change their prison keys for keys to freedom and unity, to keys of individual liberty and mass liberty, must change their keys from keys to arsenals wherein are stored those forces of destruction which they so ruthlessly unleash, and substitute for them keys to happy homes and secure cities in every land.

These same keepers of the keys are powerless to accomplish this unless the mass mind has been trained and is ready to accept its liberty. There are many of the masters of destiny whose hearts yearn with an infinite longing to undo the bonds which bind men's souls to sordidness and poverty and release them into fairer places, but they realize their helplessness and so are swept back into the vortex which moves all unseen toward the pit.

Man knows now that human life is controllable, that his destiny lies in his own hands, that the means of progression or retrogression are within his own grasp. Therefore, now is the supreme moment of life for mankind, the psychological moment in which to readjust his mind, to relate himself individually to the human race rather than to a race, group, tribe, or family. The brotherhood of man must be made a working and workable principle of international policy and this must be done at once.

This cannot be accomplished as a religious ceremonial, nor can it be accomplished through the church, nor can it be brought to fruition by any nation or group of nations. Only by the use of science and scientific principles applied by accredited scientists can this change be made. Science stands today on the pinnacle of its achievement. Its great moment has arrived, what will it do with its opportunity? Much depends upon you and me— much more depends upon you and me than anyone imagines. All that you or I can do about it is to see that our own thought meets the requirements of the new age, is adjusted to accommodate itself to the change which is coming, to see that the silent power of our own thought is directed toward and about peace and good will amongst all peoples.

Aristide Briand, foreign minister of France, said in a speech made before the veterans of the World War in France that peace would endure as long as the representatives of the nations of the world desired peace. Mr. Briand was known as Europe's "pillar of peace". It is recorded of him that, during the slaughter at Verdun, during the world war, he remarked: "I shall dedicate my future political career to the cause of maintaining peace".

France, hardest hit of any of the nations by the recent war, has discovered that peace is cheaper in dollars and cents, and that from the standpoint of the social and moral welfare of the nation there is no longer any argument about the matter. Peace must be attained and maintained, and France is going about it in the right manner. In his speech before the veterans, Mr.

Briand appealed to the women and girls and especially to the school children. In so doing he struck at the roots, at the youth and childhood of the nation, instilling into their minds the desire for peace and teaching them the mathematics of peace to the end that the future generations shall avoid war as all civilized nations now avoid contagious disease.

Mr. Briand denounced in bitter terms the old methods of settling international disputes, saying that these methods had "***covered Europe with bloody mire". News dispatches from France as this is written are filled daily with items which indicate that the best brains of that country are concerning themselves with building a national consciousness that will make war. impossible. If this is being done in France, and it is, it can be done just as intelligently and just as effectively in America. That America is a natural leader of world policies no one denies, and so America becomes the central figure in the world drama wherein peace must be exalted and peace makers honored.

History shows that man has made advancement along material, social, economic and moral lines exactly in proportion as he has improved his mental processes. His mental processes have been improved only as he has let go of old, worn-out and useless concepts and substituted for them new and workable concepts adapted to his growing condition and environment.

No man's character is larger in any way or in any of his acts than the action of his mind; likewise no nation is or can be any larger in its national concepts and national acts than its national mental acts. It behooves us all, then, to contribute our share toward the bringing into being of a new world concept; and while we all cannot be national heroes as Aristide Briand was a hero of France, we each can in his own unique way contribute his share to the national consciousness by thinking peace instead of war, by talking peace instead of war, by holding before the minds of our children the great moral characters of history for them to worship, (for childhood is hopelessly hero worshiping), by ignoring and refusing to give thought or voice to the exaltation of warriors either in our own race or any other race—to let the thought and idea of war and warriors die from the national consciousness and substitute therefore the ideas and the ideals of high and universal moral and social concept taught us by Jesus of Nazareth.

The social and moral precept he gave is in no wise complicated. It is as flexible as rubber and as strong and immovable as the mountains. Its credo is so short that any child can learn it in ten minutes, and it is: "Whatsoever ye would that men should do to you, do ye even so to them". This is not a mere platitude, it is the word description of a mental law which must be substituted for the law of "an eye for an eye" before war ceases. The most amazing discovery any one may make is that the destiny of nations does not lie in its leadership but in its individuals, that all progress is forced upon rulers by the massed demands of newly defined hopes and aspirations of their subjects.

All the ruler does is to accept the inevitable and while he poses as the ruler he knows in his heart that he is in very fact the servant of the mass.

This reveals the necessity of the individual education amongst our people, and the instant that our national consciousness rejects war, our rulers will submit to the national will. Therefore, instead of quarrelling with the ruler, or railing against the nation as it stands, be about your Father's business of perfecting your own mind and setting your own household in order.

Vox populi vox del, is true only when the idea back of the voice of the people is the voice of an idea which corresponds to the Cosmic order, the unification of humanity into one brotherhood and the promotion of individual liberty without hurt to the mass.

The Queen of Sheba might have had a sewing machine and King Solomon might have had a motor car. All the essentials and all the material were then existent but the idea was lacking. The world today might have peace, all that is lacking is the idea in the massed individual consciousness of the peoples of the world. It is your business to see that the idea of peace is established in your own mind. Mind your own business and leave others alone, but perfect your own conscience in this: peace is inevitable if civilization is to persist. Think it, teach it to your children, and *hold your peace;* that is, remain at peace, maintain peace within your own mind and affairs at any cost for it is worth whatever price you may pay for it. You are the keeper of the keys of life.

9.
Through The Law Of Love You Enter The Kingdom

THE INDIVIDUAL in learning how to handle the mental forces that surge through his mind, and sometimes leave him becalmed like a South Sea tramp steamer, at other times drive him mercilessly about like a ship in a hurricane, must understand that the conditions he seeks to relieve are not evil, unfriendly, or all-powerful. They are merely a condition which he as an individual must face intelligently and positively, applying certain definite laws to the situation.

He must realize that any household accumulates, by virtue of the fact that people live in it, a certain amount of garbage or refuse which must be disposed of that the house may be kept sanitary and livable. So, in like manner, anyone mind accumulates by virtue of the very fact of life, a certain amount of mental garbage, refuse, which must be disposed of. The Creator has not overlooked any detail of life and has placed in man's hands the tool necessary to dispose of his mental garbage.

There is nothing about which he need get emotional, there is merely some mental work to be done. Some mental garbage to be disposed of. He is to understand that the law he is to use in this mental garbage disposal is not complicated, neither is it split up into parts. It is one—one law. There is but one application possible for that law, hence there is nothing which can possibly confuse him in the application of this law and above all there is no mystery to it.

The preliminaries must be disposed of first, for if one approaches the use of psychological power in the handling of his problem with an idea that he is dealing with mystery, he will never get beyond the fact that it is a mystery, and he will never become a good workman. Nor will he succeed if he starts with the assumption that he has much to learn. He already knows all that is necessary. All he needs do is to make use of his present knowledge.

He must know that he is dealing with the kingdom of heaven and that this kingdom of heaven is the kingdom of mind and that the kingdom of mind is a place where thought is supreme in power and has no opposition.

Man in entering this kingdom of the mind needs no religion, no philosophy, no preparation, no virtue and no goodness. All he needs is his mind and he already has that. So, he is now fully equipped for the task of mental housecleaning he is to undertake.

He must know that in handling thought forces within his own mind that the Cosmic phenomenon of love is its only law, that he cannot use force, coercion or compulsion upon his thinking processes, that the idea itself is of supreme power and is equal to any task he sets it to do, and that left alone the idea will accomplish its work without the use of force, coercion or compulsion.

He must understand at once that as his mind touches upon moral questions, that morals is a personal matter, that all the moral rules ever made are wholly inadequate to solve his own personal moral problem. The proof of this lies in the fact that all the moral laws ever promulgated, pyramid like, till today, have utterly failed to solve man's moral needs. Our social condition proves it, every war proves it. The reason for this lies in the fact that all moral rules made for the multitude are of necessity all negative laws; their foundation is a negation. They are based upon, "Thou shalt not," which is itself a violation of man's primary moral need, individual liberty. All these moral laws cannot shake your own private judgment of a case. Your magistry of your own soul's welfare must ever remain within your own jurisdiction. The moralist is positively not a judge of appeal, but is of necessity an advocate before the jury of your own necessity and requirements in that moment of time.

The question is not to state the moral law to you, but the question lies in your demand as to whether or not that particular law will meet your needs, or will apply to your problem at that time.

No man ever lived who gave an adequate moral law for any man save the Carpenter of Nazareth; the moral law he gave applies to any and every moral question that may ever arise in anyone's life. It is not a rule of conduct, it is a formula of working principles wherein the individual who applies it to his moral needs finds absolute freedom of action and at the same time is apprised of the fact that if he uses that principle negatively that the law itself will demand the price of him, exact, inexorable, adequate. If he rightly applies that principle, the law itself will reward him with its blessings ... exact, inexorable, adequate.

Jesus was asked time and again to give specific moral laws in particular cases. In every case he refused to do so, refused to give any definite precept. In no case did he evade the issue, but in every instance pointed the inquirer back to the fundamental principle involved in the question itself.

If he were asked what moral law to use in the division of an inheritance, he turned the inquirer's mind back to this fundamental principle, "Whatsoever ye would that men should do to you, do ye even so to them." (Math. 7: 12) Here is the one and only possible moral law adequate for mankind. It is in no sense a negation, there is no "thou shalt not" in it, but there is a positive command, thou shalt do. There is something to be actually done in the case and what is to be done is left to the freedom of the person involved. He is given the principle—if he uses that principle negatively he knows he will pay the price, if used rightly it pays dividends.

This simple, easily remembered principle applies equally well to husband and wife, father and son, mother and daughter, mistress and maid, master and servant, sweethearts, workmen in any walk of life, to families, groups, churches, political parties, races and governments, and is the one and only moral law that will ever work and produce results.

The utter fallacy of negative moral laws lies in the fact that they immediately separate those who conform from those who cannot or will not conform, thus violating the Cosmic unity. Those who do not conform are punished, called evil, sinners, and the churches which have been the repository of morals for ages are the chief sinners in this, that they utterly repudiate the Master's teachings in this matter. Jesus taught that the way to overcome so-called evil, to transform sinners was for the good to take them into itself. Only by union or unity with goodness could evil be transformed. Yet the moralist and the church are the ones who are most loudly shouting for the punishment and crucifixion of the sinner; they demand more jails, more courts, more punitive laws every day.

The individual who seeks to apply mental power and spiritual law to the solution of his own problems, had best understand at once that in unity and unity alone lies his own salvation; that it is the joining of the two polar opposites of life which bring about the transformation so much to be desired.

To illustrate: If one is ill and his mind is filled with thoughts of pain, the one and only possible redemption for that one lies in bringing those thoughts of illness and pain into unity with thoughts of health and strength within his own consciousness. This unity of the two polar opposites must be effected in his own mind.

If one is impoverished and his mind is filled with thoughts of poverty and lack, the only solution is to think thoughts of riches and abundance. Bring these two polar opposites into unity in the mind of the thinker. I shall here restate that in dealing with such matters you are to know that you are dealing with the kingdom of mind, and that in and with mind the idea itself is supreme in power. If you start to argue with yourself or others about it, that is positively not bringing the two polar opposites together. Any sort of argument is utterly missing the mark.

If you are distressed about the moral relationships between yourself and any other one, the one and only possible solution is the application of the moral principle Jesus used; the very first thought to enter your mind in such a case would be, "If I were in his place would I like to have him butting into my affairs?" Your answer would be positively, "no". So the first thing you do with your mind is to stop making moral laws for that other one to observe. You stop picturing punishment for him. If you are distressed about the moral conduct of a loved one, the very first thing your mind will think of is to mind your own business and leave that one alone in his own inherent freedom to judge his own case and apply the best law he knows.

Every negative moral rule you or any group or any school of thought may seek to impose upon the multitudes, carries within itself the elements of its own destruction because it carries the elements of confusion and inevitably results in a moral tower of Babel.

This is true because it posits evil as a fact of being, as a specific power, and gives it a definite name and allots to it a field of activity.

If evil had any real existence, if it could stop anywhere definitely, it would destroy life itself. The fact of the matter is that man, *per se,* does not believe in evil and every effort to force a belief in evil upon mankind will fail because it is a false premise in its inception.

You cannot believe that piano strings were created and manufactured especially to create discord and to give forth the torture of discordant notes; yet, by the aid of statistics you can easily prove that the probability of discord is greater than the probability of harmony, and that for every one who can produce harmony from them there are thousands who cannot. Yet in spite of these facts and the possibility of mathematical proof of the fact, the potentiality of harmony and perfection outweighs every other consideration as well as all contradictions.

It is, therefore, more rational to let the mind dwell upon the verities of life than upon the mental distortion which apparently contradict life's inherent beauty. It is saner to learn to produce harmony than to merely strike discords ignorantly upon the mind and transmit these discords into life around us. Jesus taught us how to learn to produce harmony in life in spite of any appearance or proof of discord.

The peculiar part which Jesus Christ and his teachings plays in the world has seldom been revealed in an understandable manner to the multitude, because his teachings have been appropriated by theology and theology has confined itself to the multiplication of theories about the soul's destiny after death.

Jesus taught nothing about death—what he taught has to do with living facts, living realities—now—and has to do with the living of life for anyone at any time. No study or pondering of historical facts regarding the man or his teaching will reveal any usable truth about death to the inquirer.

All metaphysical and psychological practice turns the attention of the student toward the stillness of his own mind and away from the noise and confusion of the world about him.

It is in the realm of the inner mind that Jesus plays such an important part; Jesus, and Jesus alone of all men who ever lived, perfected his own inner consciousness; his mind is still intact, in fact and in truth he lives. He not only lives but is infinitely more alive than when he walked the earth. The fact of the actual living presence of the risen Christ must be firmly fixed in the mind of the student.

If, in going into the silence or quietly thinking, you let your mind just wander, if you merely let yourself loose in the inner realms of mind, it is but natural that those thoughts which are most familiar to you will rush in to find a resting place. This accounts for the mental confusion of most people when they first undertake to enter the silence; it is as if they were merely caught in a huge crowd of persons on the street. They get jostled and pushed about. It is necessary to have some particular objective and seek some specific place in consciousness before it is safe to undertake to enter the silence or to sit quietly and think. It is here that the living presence of Jesus Christ, the actual resurrected mind of Jesus of Nazareth, does its work for you and in you. If you think (or enter the silence) seeking him or calling his name he will respond. He knew this law and said, "Where two or three are gathered together in my name, there am I in the midst of them." (Math. 18: 20)

He meant just that. No interpretation is necessary—it means just what it says, no more, no less, "there am I in the midst."

If you will accept what he said as true, (as true as the scandal your neighbor tells you) it is as easy to get into the actual, living, loving presence of your Saviour, Jesus Christ, as it is to call upon your friend across the street and get into his actual presence. You must know your neighbor's address and you must know Jesus' address, but you know his address for he has told you what it is. "I am WITH you always"—within the inner realm of your own consciousness. You go there with your mind. You call upon your neighbor with your legs or motor car, but you call on Jesus with your mind. That is the one and only difference—the contact is sure in either case.

Also in this same inner realm of your own mind are the confused thoughts you, yourself, have generated and accepted from other confused minds. And so, when you enter the stillness of your own mind, when you enter the silence, you are mentally going out into a throng as you would if you went out on a busy street. Now, what are you seeking? If you do not know, if no one tells you whom to seek, you will find confusion multiplied. But if you are seeking Jesus Christ, the bright wisdom of his mind, the illumination of his love and presence, all you need do is to call his name and herein lies the mystery of the power of that name. Those who realize this, release a mighty power when they say: "In the name and power of Jesus Christ, be thou made whole." They are releasing the very living presence of the resurrected Christ into those words and it is not the speaker but the Christ who fulfils those words as actual manifested demonstration of healing.

This is unifying your mind with the Christ mind. It is letting the Christ mind in you solve your problems; it is the act of divine unity with the Father.

The first time you undertake this, you will feel exactly as you would the first time you called upon a stranger, rather ill at ease. But continued calling upon that person, continued conversation with him, continued communion with him develops a friendliness, a feeling of unity with him and finally you say: "So and so is a very good friend of mine."

No other person ever lived , not even your own mother, so capable of the depths of love, and possessing the supreme power to forgive and bless that lies within the power and scope of Jesus Christ.

Faith in this inner, living, presence of Jesus Christ makes you the keeper of the keys. Use of this inner presence to actually act upon your daily problems makes of you a god, a brother to him who acknowledges that he is only your elder brother, leading the way, guiding your faltering footsteps until you learn how to walk in the light alone, in the glory and majesty of your own godhood.

10.
The Secret Of Gaining A Renewed Mind

IT IS necessary for the student to know something of the mechanics of mind, and the more he understands of the mechanics of his own mental activity, the clearer will his thought be and the simpler will his thinking become and the more effective will his mental power be to act upon his outer life.

There are two modes of mechanical action in mind, both legitimate, both part and parcel of Cosmic process as relates to man, both under the direct control of man when he becomes conscious of his mental power and the supremacy of ideas in mind, and their power in the creative process which must be brought to bear upon his own estate.

Paul mentioned one specifically when he said: "Be ye *transformed* by the renewing of your mind?" The word transformed refers to that mechanical action of mind which acts to change the character of man while he lives in the body and the statement itself shows man's choice in the matter and the exact manner of procedure, for Paul continues by saying that this transformation is to be accomplished by letting the mind that was in Christ Jesus act upon your mind.

Transform, then, means to transfer. You are to transfer your mind's activity from one field of action to another field of action. You are to do this from choice, and do it consciously.

It is an unvarying law that transference of force from one field of activity to another field of activity is accomplished by what is termed affinity. Affinity and resistance are opposites, hence the teachings of Jesus are those of non-resistance. Yet resistance is perfectly legitimate and accomplishes another kind of growth in its own way but, we are now dealing with affinities.

In stating the mechanics of mind, non-resistance is the other name or term used to denote love. In using the law in the mechanics of mind we deal with affinities which are non-resistant and thus bring about a mergence or unity of two otherwise opposing forces.

First we are not to resist the mind of Christ for it has an affinity for our mind and will easily merge or form a union with our mind. It is to be accepted in love for, being an affinity, love is its only method of accomplishing those mechanics which insure union.

Now, life and every phase of life as we know it is a matter of maintaining a balance, as between the absolute and the relative, maintaining an equilibrium of both poles of being. So as we turn within to the Mind of Christ, to the Absolute, we find that the mechanics of mind, *per se* effect a union with his mind. This is the first step. We are now within, in the kingdom of the heavens, the kingdom of mind where ideas are supreme in power; here we get the clear vision, the illumination, but we must face outward again. The world of form and shape confronts us, the world of tradition, the world of fixation, the world of rules and necessity. In the first movement of our mind toward the inner realms of being, we see fulfilled the law of transformation of which Paul spoke. Our mind's activities are transferred from the without to the within. You will note that Paul said to renew our minds and this renewal caused the mind to be transformed. The mechanics of this transformation are automatic.

As we turn without, the world we see resists us, resists what our minds have accumulated by the mergence of the within; the light and glory of the indwelling Christ finds that any effort to express itself without is resisted (in our own mind).

The established habits of thoughts about persons and things resist the new impulse. Our outer mind rejects the keystone of the arch, we shout (think), "Away with it! Crucify it! It won't work! Nobody will see my point of view! I will find no sympathy with this idea, no one will understand. Why suffer, why not join the crowd and be as they are and do as they do?

"What will I get out of it anyway? What is there in it, why be different and lonely—why not be regular and get in the swim?" etc- etc. etc. *ad lib.*

Now it is right here in this mental resistance within our own minds that the possibility of our growth into the stature of Christhood is made possible. Were it not for this resistance for the Spirit within to act upon, there could be no motion, no awareness of life. Like electricity, were it not for the resistance of the filament in the lamp, there would be no light.

Moralists and theology make this ponderous error: Instead of the person acting upon his own mental resistances and thus becoming a light unto the Gentiles, he starts around the world seeking to compel others to follow rules of conduct, missing the main idea which is that the laws of Moses are to be preached to others, but the teachings of Jesus are to be preached to yourself. Never preach the teachings of Jesus to another, preach them to yourself. After they are established as habits of conduct they will show forth their works and need no preaching. The work bears witness of the fulfilment of the mechanics of mind which have brought about, first the "transformation" of the mind, and, second, the actual manifestation of that Spirit acting upon life and substance which is the divine unity, and is the use of the keystone to complete the arch of the temple wherein God is worshipped in Spirit and in truth.

Thus an understanding of the mechanics of the mind reveals that the affinity of the mind of the living Christ for our mind brings about a transference. Our thoughts are transferred from ignorance to knowledge, from hate to love, from poverty to abundance, from sin and sickness to health and wholesomeness. Then that reaction to this mechanical action of the mind brings about the completion of the transformation, for life is actually changed, fulfiling the promise: "Therefore if any man be in Christ, he is a new creature." (II Cor. 5: 17) A new creature is brought into being by this mental action of mergence, this unity of mind of man and the mind of Christ.

This is being "born again". The man has become a god.

The sinner is "saved". The blind can now "see", the leper is cleansed, the palsied now walks.

The man has become whole (holy) because he is functioning in his whole being. The Spirit of God which dwells within him is consciously known to be the animating principle of life, the source of life, Life itself; love is actually in use (action), hence no longer static as a romantic concept, but actually manifesting as an incarnation in the flesh of its spiritual quality.

The eyes see, for the mind perceives that this same principle inheres in all men. Thus love as a Cosmic phenomenon becomes natural, possible, and usable. Love is no longer restricted to me and mine, but is enlarged to include all. This is wisdom and fulfils every other law for the Cosmic phenomenon of love is the repository and the vehicle for the transmission of all law, either of the Cosmos or the individual. No man, whose mind does not consciously know the mechanics of its action in bringing about this transformation by union with the Christ Mind, can by any chance understand or become the beneficiary of love.

First we are to turn within to the living Christ. This transfers our thoughts to his thoughts, then we are to turn without and use his thoughts to act upon our own life and this accomplishes the transformation.

Thus affinity *transfers.*

Thus overcoming, the resistance *transforms.*

"To him that overcometh will I grant to sit with me in my throne." (Rev. 3: 21) So he who overcomes becomes a master.

The resistance that is to be overcome is not the resistance of another person's moral obliquity. It is the resistance of our own moral nature that is to be overcome by the mergence of our mind with the mind of our own indwelling Christ.

You are not charged with saving the world — that is Christ's job. He has assumed the responsibility for this, and he is quite capable of fulfilling His mission.

I am personally quite familiar with the mechanics of mind as stated above, for I have practiced with them until results have proven them to be immutable and the transformation, while in no wise complete, is far enough advanced to be perfectly identifiable as the effects of the contact, of the action of Christ's inviolable love, of the healing and soothing grace of his truth. To him I commend you—and may his peace rest upon you now and forevermore.

* * * *

And so, beloved fellow-journeyer, I have sought to use my feeble, flickering light to show you the way to the great Light, even the Light of the Christ within you, to the end that you may be born again, that you may enter into the Light and walk no more in darkness, to the end that the glory of God may be made manifest in you, in wholeness, in health and abundance, in joy and in every good work.

Of St. John it was said: "He was not that Light, but was sent to bear witness of that Light. That was the true Light, which lighteth every man that cometh into the world." That Light burns brightly within your mind—

now—in the kingdom of heaven within you, and that Light is the living, radiant presence of the resurrected Christ of God.

Religious ecstasy, emotional ecstasy, mass psychology will not, so far as I know, reveal this Light to you. Calm, sane, quiet, persistent thought of and about and toward the truths that Jesus taught, *will* reveal that Light to you. The method of approach is contained within this book; if you have failed to see it, read the book again and again. It is here and you will find it if you search diligently for it.

You will search diligently for it if you are really seeking the Light.

"I AM" the Keeper of the Keys.